M000081571

*Dinner with Emerson*

*Dinner with Emerson*

poems by

Wendy Mnookin

Tiger Bark Press  *  Rochester, New York  *  2016

Copyright © 2016 by Wendy Mnookin. All rights reserved. No part of this work may be reproduced in any technology or format without written permission from the publisher, except by a reviewer.

Published by Tiger Bark Press,
202 Mildorf Ave., Rochester, NY 14609.

Designed by Philip Memmer.

Cover art by Anthony Ulinski, "Empty Chair #2," 2007, oil and wax on canvas.

Author photo by Sharona Jacobs.

ISBN-13: 978-0-9860445-9-5

# *Contents*

*for my mother*
*Marjorie Reiss Miller*
*1923-2015*


*and for my grandchildren*
*Max Theodore, Eliza Reiss, and Lucy Wren*

*He wished this month had a less military verb for a name.*
*Why March? How about a month named Skip? That could work.*

—Lorrie Moore, "Debarking"


*Unicorns are really real.*
*Paleontologists just haven't discovered them yet.*

—Max Mnookin

*Spring*

## How the Day Begins

At night the cat
chooses a place on the bed
and settles in, head

tucked into paws,
small engine of purrs
radiating heat.

If, during the night,
the woman leaves the bed
for a drink of water,

if the man gets up to pee,
the cat won't move. The woman,
or the man, has to find a way back,

some arrangement of arms
and heart that leaves the puzzle
undisturbed. And in the morning,

when the cat wakes, when she
sneezes once, and again,
when she arches her back

and pads from the bed, she steps
delicately on the man's chest,
the woman's closed eyes.

# 4 A.M.

This is for her exhaustion.
This is for the tea I brew, *Mother's Milk,*
with fennel and coriander and blessed thistle.

This is for the baby, burping and puckering
and now slowing down, mouth slack at her breast.

It's too soon for him to sleep—
she flicks her finger on his heel.
He sucks. He sleeps.

This is for touch and taste,
the smell of his scalp like hay
when she gives him to me to rock.

This is for me, rocking my own child
by a window's slivered view—
if I craned my neck I could just see the river,
inky, shadowed—spit-up on my sleeve
and dreams in the pocket of my flannel robe.

# First Child

Shouts of girls playing soccer
in the field below, a spring so sassy
and sure. Flagrant crocuses, resolute
tulips. The dark bulk of my doctor

shadowing the door. *Maybe she'll do better
in the delivery room,* he says to a nurse.
*Better* isn't enough. I want to be his best girl,
the one who delivers her baby without fuss

or bother. He taps his pipe against a table
where ice chips melt in a paper cup.
Who is that person who grabs for the mask—

*precious savior, sweet oblivion—*
when he says I can have it?
The second hand on the clock refuses.

# Fax from My Son

I turn the fax one way, then another,
but I can't decipher
these mysterious bubbles and smudges.
Even when I read *Happy Mother's Day*
I don't understand

and then I do—
                    I run outside,
where you're attaching
new windshield wipers to the car,
and wave the paper in your face,
jumping up and down
while you figure out

you're looking at an ultrasound
of our grandchild. Oh

isn't it all worth it
to come to this place together
where the people we love most
are the same people,

where you can say, brushing
sweat from your eyes,
*We have new wipers*
*for the next downpour,*

and I can say,
*You really should have*
*pulled over back there,*
*we couldn't see a thing.*

## Grandson, Just Born

Fastened around your naked chest
and plugged to the nearest outlet,
a neon blanket breaks down
the bilirubin your body can't.
I hold you, and walk the distances
allowed by the cord, your body
curling into mine. *Listen.*
While you still understand
through touch and heartbeat,

I want to tell you this—
in the worst times,
when two wings of rage
smudged your father's cheeks,
when a phone ringing at night
tumbled me into freefall,
this was also true: his fingernails
grew their heart-shaped moons.
His collarbones managed.
His elbows refused to give in.
And his soul, hidden away and still,
his soul was a meteor. Bright. Hard.

# Chimes

The cat wanders in and out, interested
in a theoretical, cat-like way. The dog
settles in, watchful, as my daughter paces
through the first hours of labor. Miles away,

where I wait, my grandmother's clock
marks time, a single chime on each half hour,
the hours numbered in deep bass throbbing.
I fix tea. I do laundry. I fold laundry.

I turn the pages of a book: in Convent San Marco
a single fresco is painted on the walls of each cell.
A single fresco to contemplate for a lifetime.
What would that be like, to inhale

blood red flowers, the folds of Mary's dress,
the terrible glow lighting her face and hair?
I wanted to be with my daughter,
but she wanted calm in the room and said *no.*

# My Grandmother's Clock

### i

On my hands and knees
I'm working my way
up the tall clock, trying
to get a grip on those tricky surfaces
before the chimes start.
I keep falling back.
The flat white face couldn't care less.
*Hello!* I call, too heartily.
Way too heartily.

### ii

5 a.m., and you leave to catch a plane.
*Shhh.* It's enough
the birds are announcing
their complicated biographies.
They trill the hard parts, so certain
someone is listening.

### iii

I bury my head under a pillow,
curl onto my side of the bed.
I wake to find myself
stretched across space,
arms flung wide.

*iv*

Nurses hovered over my mother.
She was going to get better.
I ran the hospital hall, down
and back, and again, and again.
Footsteps kept my mother breathing.

*v*

Am I too old to be fed,
spoonful by spoonful,
soup from a blue-rimmed cup?
Curtains resist the breeze.
The cup in my hand shivers.

*vi*

There is so little left
and yet ants have found
an edge of fallen apple.
My work lies untouched, hazy
in the middle distance. Outside,
the startling red of a cardinal
assaults newly green leaves.
Windows long
for an ending, lyric, closed.

## Crimson Peonies

In from the garden with an armful
of peonies, I stand on a stool, peering

into shelves for a missing blue vase.
It's not behind the rooster pitcher,

jaunty and crowing, or the wedding bowl,
bride and groom winding

a hopeful processional. It's not
behind the cheese grater,

the lettuce spinner, a knife sharpener
I've never used. Who even needs

a colander with a missing leg,
five unmatched espresso cups?

The crush on my shelves
must be hiding that vase—

things don't just vanish, do they—
and now my friend's kiln-fired mug

with the perfectly balanced handle
falls from my hand and bursts

into shards, jagged and unforgiving,
vase still hidden, nothing

about to be found
or mended or made whole.

## Taffeta. Lipstick. Stockings.

My gym, all gussied up with ribboned garlands,
balloons hanging from rafters, paper lanterns.
The punch bowl with its plastic ladle, the fizzy
and the startling, every bite of cake and too
sweet icing. The deep bass moving from slow
to fast and back to slow again. Staccato
laughter. A few brave couples dancing
in the free-throw lane. Our hands
around each other's waists, girls bent close
with secrets. My just-washed hair electrified
with a thousand-and-one possibilities—
cheek and shoulder. Breath. Hip. Knotted
thighs. Those boys who used to be friends,
who used to choose me for dodgeball, now
utterly other, sharp and exotic, menthol-tinged
and splashed with clove, with the cool burn of panic.

# Frankincense

*after "Girl Reading" by Edmund Tarbell*

She pushes her chair away from the desk—
not the comfortable chair, no,

the ladder back—and begins again
the book that swims on the tide

of her attention. The letter
recedes, and the pen, the desk

on its four strong legs, the fringed
floor, all swallowed by darkness,

while her body is funneled by light
that seems to pour at the window

but really escapes from the book. Don't
be fooled by her demure collar,

the pliant curve of her back.
Hers is life grasped greedily,

what she reads revealing her
to herself, all *horseback*

and *cobblestone, thistle* and *myrrh,*

*candle wax, bee balm,* the letter
composed now, linear, shadowed,

faithful, none of it easy.

# Russian Novel

I watched from a window
as kids careened through the yard,
playing games whose rules I didn't get.
Parents stood around in knots of conversation,
drinking beer from the cooler, or wine
in plastic cups. Potato chips were crushed
into the lawn. Was it July 4th?
I was helping my friend in the kitchen—
slicing carrots and celery, organizing
mustard and relish and ketchup—
when she wiped her hands on her apron
and gave me a push. *Enough,* she said.
*Go on outside with the others.*
I saw her husband laying coals
for the fire—he would die in two years,
but that was a distant future
we knew nothing about. It was an hour,
at least, till dinner. An hour.
I topped off my wine
and went—quietly, so she wouldn't notice—
to the study, where I settled in the blue armchair.
I took my Modern Library *Anna Karenina*
from the diaper bag and entered again
her world—love abandoned for passion,
love abandoned for death. Later
they sent my son to find me.
*Mommy, Mommy,* he cried,
tugging my arm.

# High Heels

My mother poured herself a drink,
still in her coat. She sank back
into the couch and kicked
off her shoes, one, and then the other.
She closed her eyes.

I studied the bar cart
with its tall bottles and squat bottles
and those tiny bottles filled with green.
I studied the shoes
that matched her dress

and kicked off my scuffs
and put on those heels,
lurching around the coffee table,
head high, shoulders back.
My mother opened her eyes

and for long minutes said nothing.
I thought she might yell at me.
Then she went back to her drink.
*Keep them,* she said.
*You'll get better with practice.*

## Storm

Sighing
down their branches

willows weep

what's hidden.
Catkins

mouth the need

for wind. Bark
furrows, wanting

touch, not wanting it.

# Summer

# *Still Life*

The ground allows
a trickle of water. The sun,
busy being syrupy

and benign, lazes
toward pears
warming in the window.

It's all tied together—
sorrow drinks
at the stream, pears

ripen. Your neck
tastes of honey, *honey*
easy on the tongue,

*sweetheart,* deer
at the salt lick, head
raised, still. I'm trying

to make sense
of what came before,
before I keep on.

# Boardwalk Rhapsody

My father and I
stroll by the sea.
He's in a white suit.
I'm the child
in a lavender dress tied with a sash.
There's a teahouse, and all that
impossibly blue sky.

If I'm not dreaming
I have to consider
what I'm doing
on a Sunday afternoon
on a boardwalk I've never seen
with a father who died.

I run on ahead, enchanted
by sparkle and spray.
He calls me *Sweetheart*
holding out his arm
for my hand to rest on, lightly.

He steers me toward a table
(what is a teahouse, exactly?)
shielded from sun,
just barely,
by an umbrella with fat swaying tassels.

On the table
a pitcher, still empty,
and a jar of honey.
Bees hover.
I am with him
(what is a father, exactly?)
and I wait.

# Monday Morning

Go ahead, the Past shrugs.
Use Monday as a springboard.

Get up early, grab
a brisk walk around the reservoir.

While I'm huffing along the trail
the Past, dressed in lazy tatters,

waits at the door, smoking
a Lucky Strike and all

caffeined up. Who
smokes anymore, anyway?

The Past, which has nothing
to lose, everything

scattered and done,
years ago. *It's a new day,*

I breathe. *A new day,*
*a new day.*

The Past practically chokes,
he's laughing so hard.

## Central Park

A father and his little girl burst
from *Via Quadronno,* a wave of coffee
following. They speak to each other

in the musical tone of a language
I almost understand as he bends down
to fasten her sun hat, cupping her chin,

careful of the soft skin.
I envy her that touch, turn
toward the park, past houses

trailing ivy, doors preening brass.
My grandfather used to walk me
to this park, slow and stately

among the Sunday fathers.
He wore a fedora. He carried a cane.
There was a tunnel where we shouted

our names, walls echoing back.
Once he bought me a salted pretzel.
Once he bought me a blue balloon.

It slipped the knot on my wrist
and drifted into sky. He let me call him
*Pa,* as close as I could come to *Father.*

# Mornings

Mother napped in the bedroom
while I stayed quiet with Grandpa in the living room,
divided in two by a curtain—
one side for me and Grandpa, all set up with his bed
and a table and chairs,
the other for Grandma Hattie, so she could work.
The doorbell rang
and she opened the door and I heard shuffling and talking
and I wanted to look.
Grandpa said *No, she is making her patients feel better.*
I sat on his bed
while he read the paper, pushing his glasses up on his nose
and making sucking sounds
through his teeth. Every once in a while he patted my head,
a little surprised to see it was me.
Lunchtime Grandma Hattie pulled back the curtain
with its magic wand
and disappeared into the kitchen that fit one person at a time.
She made Grandpa red soup
with a circle of sour cream on top. She made Mother a sandwich
with a toothpick holding it together
which Mother said was *too much food.* And for me a hard-boiled egg
with raisin eyes
and carrot curl hair and a ruffled lettuce skirt. That egg
looked like it wanted to dance.
After lunch Grandma Hattie and I walked to the bakery
where I got a cookie
with a thumbprint of jam in the middle. *The air
is good for you,* she said,
pinching my cheeks to get the roses back.

# *Hopscotch*

Chalk softening in my hand,
I scratch a grid onto asphalt,
marking off squares, a crowning
dome. Numbers come last.

And then I stand completely
still. Trees fling their acorns.
Clouds scud through sky.
Kids shout *oley oley in free.*

Let babies cry—who knows
what might follow a girl
whose stone lands right,
who balances on one foot.

Who doesn't touch a single line.

# I'm Sorry

I draw a line down the center of the room—
an imaginary line only I can see—
and don't let my sister step across it.
And the toys are on my side.

I read *Bambi* under the covers
with my Brownie flashlight
when I'm supposed to be sleeping.

I read *Bambi* under the covers
and his mother dies
and he gets shot and has to walk in circles
to confuse the hunters until the bleeding stops.

I lean too far out over the railing by the river.

Mother takes me to the dentist
but there's nothing wrong with my teeth.
*You are making your teeth ache,* the dentist says,
*by not letting the tears out.*

I lean too far out over the railing by the river
till the tugboat horn echoes in my chest.

I stare—it's rude to stare—
at the boy jumping from stone to stone
at Boat House Pond. His mother
runs behind, *Stop! Come Back!*
windmilling her arms. He stops
and sticks out his tongue.
Inside my head *I'm sorry.*

# Beans

Some are easy to reach, brazen, ripe
and ready. Others hide behind clenched leaves,
unwilling. I find them by feel,

fingers searching, snapping them from the vine.
Breathing their smell, keen, almost bitter,
I carry them in, cut the ends on a scarred

wooden board. When I blanch them
in boiling water, steam rising to fog the kitchen
on a day that's reaching for the 90s,

I tie on a bandana to keep sweat
from stinging my eyes. And then the beans
need an hour, in this humidity I give them two,

till they've dried on the counter
and I can pack them in bags, sealed
and labeled for the freezer.
                            What a harvest.

Right here in Newton. I stand back,
survey my labor—*Green Beans, 08/10.*
Oh, what harm have I ever done?

# Favorite Uncle

Our favorite uncle, Stanley,
the youngest of five brothers
and the most handsome,

used to play a game with my sister
and me, hiding a nickel
and making us choose

which hand, clenched behind his back,
held the prize. The two of us
danced from one foot

to the other, giddy with wanting—
the nickel, of course, and also
the wide smile, the bear hug

the winner got from Uncle Stanley.
But I remember, even in the heat
of his attention, how winning

hurt a little, my sister
completely still, blinking hard.
Uncle Stanley had no children.

For twenty years he loved a woman
who was married to someone else.
And when he finally married her

we didn't love him quite as much.
He was our same gallant uncle
but distant now, distracted by having

what he could no longer long for.

# Questions, 1969

Huge and unembarrassed, my friend
floated like a Buddha in the small pool.
I drank iced tea, graded
chlorine-splashed papers
on *The Mayor of Casterbridge.*

When she had her baby
on a bed covered with a shower curtain,
I did what I was told, sealed
the placenta in a plastic bag,
stashed it in the freezer.

Life was breathless in its daring
or boring in its routine. Newly married,
I loved a man so desperate
for his young son back east
he cried in my arms.

I wanted to miss someone
that much. I quit my job,
sold my yellow Mustang.
Divvied up the wedding gifts,
some of them unopened.

Did she plant the placenta under a tree?
Had I ever mourned my father?
How much could I miss
a husband I so easily walked out on?

# Constellations

I lie in a hammock, sweating
glass of tea pressed to my forehead,
while somewhere down the street

a ball pounds on asphalt,
clatters against a backboard.
Shouts skid on humid air,

someone cheers, someone's
missed a shot. Do I miss
that noise and chaos, my kids

playing *Horse* in the driveway,
*Mother-May-I* on the lawn?
*If you lose by one, you still lose.*

The dog running circles, trying to herd,
barking her frantic commands.
*Please,* they'd beg

when I called them for dinner,
*just a few more minutes.*
And really, what do I care?

Let them play until it's too dark
to see. Let them play
forever, refusing

to come in until the stars come out,
Lyre, Eagle and Swan, bright
burn in summer's nostalgia.

# Crane's Beach

It's all here, waiting for me.
Bright blast of sun on water.
Tug of sand as waves pull out,
and how quickly the grandchildren
return as waves crash in.

Someone's always selling ice
in paper cups. Someone's
always selling lures. And down the beach
someone's waving to a stretch of ocean
though I see no one.

Waves sulky now, and salt
so likely to sting. Less likely (but still!)
to drown. And me here to shelter
any child, damp and hot and
pinkly peeling, hard up against my knee.

## Another Last Summer

Though I don't believe
the hard-boiled dialogue,
though motivation's hazy

and character sketched
with lipstick smudge and
coffee stain, who cares?

Give me a thirty-eight
snuggled in an ankle strap,
give me a tow-headed

five-year-old, snatched
from the bus stop, shenanigans
that rob an elderly widow

of her entire life
savings. Give me bourbon
and *Gitanes,* a cryptic

dress, clingy and cut
down to here. Take
your day lilies, greenly

ecstatic. Who needs to be
reminded we are not
born again each year?

# Lizard

She folds her hands on the table.
She won't take a drink.
Too easy for her to finish the bottle,
and another,
and soon it won't be a problem anymore.
Depending on what you think *it* is.

I really want a drink.

*Have you noticed,* she says,
her fingers twining and releasing,
*there's always someone who uses the word "moment"?*
Not me.

Though as soon as I say this, I think of lizards,
those delicate orange ones, completely still
when I come across them on the trail,
as if frozen, or suspended,
and then, in the next moment,
faster than seems
possible, gone.

# *Chipmunks*

They go after my Sungold tomatoes, richly sweet,
small orange clusters just the right height
for my grandchildren's eager hands. From a maze
they've dug they come and go, a head appearing

first at one hole, then another. If they see me—
smell me?—they disappear. It's only if I'm
perfectly still, and downwind, that I catch them
in the act. And with what finesse a chipmunk

holds a tomato between its paws, spits out the skin,
spits out the small black seeds. Sweeping away
the leavings, I lack all finesse, blustery
and awkward with rage. At the theft, yes,

and also at how adorable they are, popping up
from underground, ears pricked, whiskers astir.
How can I pack their tunnels with dirt?
Their babies are no bigger than my thumb.

What now, I think, violins? No, it's a chorus of cicadas
insisting on their own brief lives. In my next life
I'll be a rock at the bottom of a bucket of rocks,
weighted there, sure of my place in the pail.

# Long Shadows

I'm dreaming myself into shadows
of late afternoon, their myriad evocations,
when two slatted wooden chairs take shape.

Adirondack chairs, red and ardent yellow.
Is that a child leaning from a chair?
Someone has pulled her hair too tight.

I didn't want to. I only wanted to
run my fingers through the whorl
of everything. I wanted everything,

which was maybe too much.
Why is it shadows reach for me
while the chairs, those sturdy chairs,

fade into inconsequence? Out walking
this morning before sun-up,
I was sluicing through fog so thick

street signs vanished. Bungalows.
Honey locusts tangled into nothingness.
What a fury of intention shadows hide.

## Midsummer Opera

In the middle of the night, the heart insists. It's lonely
lying here next to you, listening as you breathe your day
into dream's exotic hieroglyphs. *Bon Appetit!* sang Julia Child.
We smiled and ate cupcakes, licking icing from our lips.
The scrim of sugar made promises. With everything at stake

I let the sun, on its own, come up, the shiny new teapot
shriek from the stove. Metal turns a livid blue, insisting,
as water slithers away, unnoticed, uncared. And me,
gone into a book, the creak of my chair, that bright place
between absence and return, self possession the only currency.

*Fall*

# Fault Lines

Words
splinter into reflections

I stitch into smoke.
Into ice for my drink.

What I mean is
smoke shreds. Ice melts.

What I mean is
what, and to whom,

and do I own
or owe anything

with filigree, fancy
or fact? Lacy words

drape in my drawer,
racy words splurge

on my pillow. I keep them
skewed across a bed

in a way only possible
when you sleep alone.

I keep them on edge
like the salty taste of sweat,

bug bites scratched
well and good. Raised welts,

blood. And still the itch.
I rake the words into piles.

I scatter them and start again,
pressing the best

like petals in a diary,
where I keep them

scented, tinted, tethered,
layered, savored,

taunted, tallied, too
tender, too young to be done.

## As the Fog Burns Off

Outlined in quick black pencil,
the woman I draw
stares at the river. I leave her

unfinished. She's still
the creamy white of paper
but she will not last

like that. Soon
she'll be bathed
in background, circling

gulls, sweetly muscled men
robed in deep blue-green.
While one element turns

into another, they bend
to a net on the far shore.
How can a river mean

what it says, flooded
with sails, with longing?
How to tell things apart,

river, men, gulls, net,
and the woman, stippled
as she is, shadow

of all my disappearances.

## The Print above My Bed

They don't look like tea bags.
More like intricate fossils,
or bird bones set in shifting sand,
edges wavy, not quite fixed.

Mornings the artist would brew her tea
then stamp the damp tea bag
onto thick creamy paper,
day after day,
nine across, thirteen down.

In bed for the third week, I take my time
with catalogs, thumbing through pages,
folding corners. I decide
on sheets, Scandinavian sunshine
with sprawling orange flowers.
*Backordered,* says a voice on the phone.

*You don't understand,* I nearly cry.
*I need those sheets.*

# Cats

The child is allergic.
They must give the cats away.
Oh which should she give up first,
and how far, and how long?
*All?* she asks.
*Yes, all.* And so

she forgets her slippers,
pink, with sequins, when she hurries
to Slipper Day at school.
They wait all day on the counter, abandoned
with a few soggy Cheerios,
hardening crusts of toast.

One by one the cats come home—
the decree lifted—
moody, demanding
bits of turkey, a shoulder to knead.
They wrap themselves
around chair legs, her legs,
purring loudly.

And though her mother says
everything will be fine—
which means everything
will be forgotten—
the child refuses ice cream
and keeps her losses close.

No: she eats the ice cream,
chocolate and vanilla both,
and keeps her losses close.

# The Gods

He spins and spins me
till, released, I stumble forward,
arms outstretched, clutching

a donkey's tail. My friends
squeal and shout, *Over there!*
*Over there!* as I stagger blindly—

but not quite.
We have a secret, don't we,
my stepfather and I—

a thin slit of light
at the bottom of the blindfold
lets me find my way

and slap the tail on the donkey.
I'm only a little scared
when the lights go out

and Mother appears
with an iced pink cake,
candied flowers wavering

in the flame of seven candles,
one to grow on.
It takes a lot of breath

to blow them out,
almost more
than I have. Mother

leans close. *Make a wish,*
she says. Would a dog
be too much? My stepfather

points the camera's eye
right at me. I close my eyes
tight. Oh I want

to be on their team.
I want to wave a banner
and cheer for them,

this man and this woman—
not a real banner, made of cloth
and tied to a pole.

You knew that, didn't you?
That the banner wasn't real?

# Arrivals

### i

Roy Rogers chases bad guys
right off the TV screen
while I eat greedy mouthfuls
of peanut butter from a spoon.
Why can't I have riding lessons?
They give them in Central Park.

### ii

My stepfather stamps his shoes
at the door, leaving
big wet footprints.
He comes to me, holding
open the pocket of his overcoat
so I can reach the caramel inside.

### iii

I believed he wrote messages,
as a boy, on birch bark. No matter
that he grew up on asphalt
streets in Brooklyn. I gave him
a childhood in forests.
I gave him moccasins and stealth,
knowledge of plants and trees.
I was sure he could put up a teepee,
find clear running water.

*iv*

When Roy is crawling through smoke
to rescue a child from a burning barn,
when Trigger gallops full out,
rushing them to safety
as burning timbers fall,
I don't have time for a caramel.

# Departures

### i

An odor I can't name
clings to my stepfather's sheets.
Sweet, cloying.
When I hold his hand, the mark
my thumb makes on his skin
takes a long time to fade.

### ii

He married my mother
when I was four.
When they asked
*Who takes this man—*
I shouted, *Me!*

### iii

I open the window.
Mother comes in
and closes the window.

### iv

The first time he yelled at me—
a small offense, I was bouncing around
in the back seat of the car,
he told me to sit still—
a space opened in my chest,
clattery and uncontained.

*v*

He used to dance me around the room,
my bare feet clinging to his shoes.
*You look like Grace Kelly,* he told me.
That was when Grace Kelly looked like a princess.
Before she was a princess.

# Lullaby

The grass grows, uncut, promissory.
The sky is careful, only
fragments of humming break through.

Not yet steady on her feet, Eliza
concentrates on planting each foot,
swaying a little as she offers raisins
to the open mouths of flowers.
If she drops one, she picks it up
and tries again.
This is serious business,
the feeding of flowers.

I keep secrets because I must—
bees are dwindling,
and without them
the apple tree has stopped
making apples.

Who could tell a child such a thing?
This is not the world we meant to give her.

# Why Is This Night Different?

While his sister lies sick
I give my grandson what I know
he loves—apple juice in a sippy cup,
soft scrambled eggs. She's going
to get better, everyone says so,
but there's his father, manic
with responsibility, and his mother,
puking from a hospital-borne bug,
and me, wanting to dye my hair purple,
throw a glass against the wall
and then, on hands and knees,
search for each shard and sliver,
anything to be swept
into some other drama.
I wait for Max to ask for *More,*
*Dita, more,* more egg, more juice,
more frontloader and backhoe
on the pages of his truck book—
he's two, what can he know?—
but he stares into distance
and carefully, so carefully,
rests his head on the eggs
and sighs himself to sleep.

# Hoopla

Leaves never asked
for honky-tonk orange,
yellow's wide wonder.
They quiver and wait
for night, garish
scarlet dream, a smell
of burning. At dawn,
flung on the grass
with all those droplets
of dew, each one
waving a ticket,
leaves say it straight—
a rising sun isn't all
promise. Also heat,
and quickly drying air.

*Winter*

# Waking

Some days it's feet to the floor
and into slippers and day's begun.
Some days I clutch my pillow, clinging
to dream's humid boundaries. Some days
when I settle my granddaughter Lucy
in her car seat and kiss her good-bye
she's already rubbing her blanket
on her cheek. One day I woke on the grass,
thrown from the car. My mother lay
on the road, bleeding from her head.
My father moaned. Lucy
woke in Vermont to pine trees
laced with snow, cold she could taste
when she breathed. *Where's Dita?*
she cried. *You'll see your grandma soon,*
my daughter said, holding her
to her shoulder, stroking her hair.

## My Mother Calls, Again

My mother calls, again, to tell me
how wonderful her friends' daughters are

and what did she do to end up
so neglected? I refill my coffee,

swirling the milk with extra care.
I eat my toast, wetting

the tip of my finger to get
every last crumb. By the time she's done

I've forgotten the apple cake
baking in the oven

and have to crack a window
against the smell of burnt cinnamon.

And here comes
wind chill, followed

by news from the universe,
gears grinding on the mail truck.

Who's that behind the wheel?
I'm scraping blackened apple from the pan

while this stranger rubs his forehead
in the off-kilter way of an eighth-grade boy,

stabbing me with his awkward hopefulness.
*Hi, I'm Jackson,* he calls,

but I won't be swayed—
I want my regular mailman.

I take the envelopes, take the bright,
useless flyers. Turn back

to my kitchen, where I slam and clatter,
spill my coffee, scare the cat.

# Dream of Snow

My children abandon the car
and start walking, a semaphore of scarves
bright against winter's blank stare.

My scarf is more Isadora Duncan.
I pirouette and leap, hoping for a different ending

as they get smaller, disappearing into drift.

They don't think I can
and then I do, huffing and puffing
to blow the drifts down.
They have to change their opinion of me,
slowly, a decade at a time.

# Woolen Hat

On Tuesdays I pick up Max at preschool
and strap him in his car seat
and drive him to my house
and give him a snack and he plays
with his trains in the basement
and then I strap him in his car seat
and we go to yoga for 4-year-olds
and then I strap him in his car seat
and bring him back to my house
and fix him dinner—*can I just
eat something that's already cooked?*—
and I clean up after dinner and give him
his bath, with bubbles, and brush his teeth
and read him 3 train books and take him
back to the bathroom for a last pee
and rub his back and sing
*This Land Is Your Land*
till he settles down and sleeps
and then he calls me at 1 because
he can't find Lambie, she must have
fallen out of bed, and he calls me at 5—
*is it wake-up time?*—and at 6
we pad to the kitchen together
for breakfast—*I like my muffin
frozen*—and I make his snack for school
and I make his lunch for school
and I get him dressed—*I always wear my pj's
under my clothes*—and out the door
and strapped into his car seat
for the drive back to school

and at the good-bye door
I give him 5 hugs and a big kiss
and head straight to Dunkin' Donuts
for a large coffee. At home, settled
with the newspaper, I see his woolen cap,
left behind, white with blue stripes.
He might need that hat.
Though the day's gotten warmer,
and he hates hats, they're itchy,
it's possible, isn't it,
he might need that hat?
That he might need me
to take the hat to him?

# And Anyway

It's so cold the air hurts my teeth.
Max takes shallow breaths,
claps his mittened hands.

I'm trying to pay attention
to his chatter, but I'm distracted
by the cable stitch of ice on pine needles,

by sun cutting light
through the clean fabric of sky.
I don't know, really,

what the sky is made of,
except, in a general sense, air.
Whether it has any kind of end

or beginning. I'll have to
look it up. Max stamps his boots
on hard pack snow. *Just guess,*

he says, hands on hips,
the littlest warrior. *Just guess.*
He digs at the frozen crust

and manages to shape a ball
that he hurls with a pitcher's wind-up
against a tree. *And anyway,* he says,

pleased with the satisfying splat,
*I'm going to know you my whole life.*
He runs ahead, leaning into winter.

*Just because you have white hair,*
he shouts in my direction,
*doesn't mean you're old enough to die.*

# Three Lives

In Paris, Ernest Hemingway
and Hadley put their cat in the crib
to babysit their son. The streets
were noisy with dancing.
They had drinking to do.

They had lives.
This morning my mother
calls from New York,
crying. Her calendar's gone.
How will she fill the spaces

of her days? On the phone
I walk with her from room to room.
*Henry!* she cries, when she finds
the cat curled on her calendar.
When my cat got old she peed

on the rug. Not just any rug.
My grandmother's oriental.
One day she looked at me with big eyes
and peed on the couch.
I took her to a vet. *Forgive yourself,*

she said, when I put the cat down
and went home and sat by a window
trying to wish a bird to the feeder.
Between this life and the next,
there is no space to hide.

## Without Dog

She won't eat,
drinks only small
sips from the bowl I hold
out to her.

*Please,* I say, *please.*
She attends earnestly,
panting, watching the air.

~

I learn to stick the needle
quickly. I learn
to do it in the dark.

One hand holds an IV bag
high, for pressure,
the other slips the needle in.

~

After a week
she walks again,
around the block,
to the school yard.

No rules now—
I feed her hot dogs.
I feed her chicken fingers.

She runs in the woods.

~

And then one day
she won't lie down, won't
rest her head between her paws.

When I reach to stroke her
she startles and pulls away.
She keeps herself alert,
head raised, listening,
till she falls into an exhausted sleep

~

from which she wakes
to stagger around the room,
listing to one side,
bumping into walls.

*Do you want to go outside?*
I say. I say,
Let me give you the world.

~

UPS leaves a yellow slip on the door,
*Sorry we missed you.*
I stick it on the fridge

and when it falls to the floor
the sound of paper
fluttering

~

makes me turn and think
*She's back.*

~


I dream her young
and healthy
but still
she hesitates, outside
a dog door we never had

until she gathers herself
and leaps, landing

in our kitchen.
She scrapes her nails across the floor,
turns
and tries it again
and again,
what a show-off,
out, in—I can watch

forever, her body
poised
for the jump, then
launched, ears flapping—

out, in,
out.

# Nights

Mother in the next bed cried into her pillow
so no one would hear.
But I did hear, and so did Grandma Hattie,
who climbed out of our bed,
tucking me back in. *Shhh,* she said, smoothing my bangs—
we were going to cut them
when we had time—and then she went to Mother's bed
and helped her up.
She put her arm around Mother's waist, and Mother leaned
against her, and they walked
and walked, to the door, to the window, to the statue
that looked like a lion
but Grandma Hattie said was a panther and they don't have panthers
around here. Back and forth they walked
Grandma Hattie saying words I couldn't quite hear,
while in the living room
Grandpa slept behind a curtain that divided the room in two.
I tried to stay awake
to see what would happen, but it was like a lullaby,
their footsteps on the floor,
Grandma Hattie's words, the snoring and coughing
of the oxygen tank
from the other room, and under it all
Mother crying.
Sometime in the night Grandma Hattie got back in bed with me.
Sometime Mother fell asleep,
a pillow pressed to her cheek. The room got light. The oxygen tank
stuttered through another night.

# Questions, 1959

Grandma Julie had a parakeet
named Pretty Boy. *I love you, Wendy,*
he said. *I love you, Wendy.*
I knew she taught him this
but it seemed to me he really did.

Grandma Julie had pillows piled on her bed,
lace pillows and velvet pillows
and pillows with embroidered flowers.
She had curtains that went down and down
and finished in a puddle on the floor.

Grandpa Herman was dead
and still the curtains smelled like his pipe.
*He died of a broken heart,* Mother said,
*after your father died.* When I slept over
I pushed the pillows off the bed

to make room. I lay there, listening
to the breath of the gas burner,
Grandma Julie making tea. I missed
Pretty Boy, who flew out a window
*to be with the other birds.*

Was he happy living with the other birds?
Whose hands were carved in the headboard,
holding each other tight?
How do you die of a broken heart?

## My Mother Turns Ninety

She's so thin her wedding ring
slips off her finger and she begins

passing it from one hand to the other.
She says she wants to move my father's grave

so she can be buried between
both her husbands. Really?

My father died at 29.
In the house of my childhood

there wasn't one photo of him,
not on a bureau, not on a desk,

not in the picture case in her wallet.
He was a secret saved for night,

when she sat on my bed and rubbed my back,
whispering stories—

she met him when he was a lifeguard,
*all the girls wanted him,*

they drove through the night to see the sunrise
from the Brooklyn Bridge. *Richard,*

she called him, and I did, too.
Her next husband I called Father

for fifty years. From the street below
car lights beckon

like a movie scene. Here in the apartment
I'm lulled by the back-and-forth,

the slight pause of the ring
as it settles in her palm

before the gold darts, again,
to the other hand.

# *At Twelve*

I don't know how I figured out
about those pills. Maybe I asked her.
Maybe Mother thought it was best
to be honest. Or maybe she didn't
say a word and neither did I.
I didn't take one every day. Only
once in a while I went to her bathroom
casually, as if I might be looking
for shampoo, or Cashmere Bouquet powder,
and slipped a pill in my bathrobe pocket.
Red if I wanted to be knocked out.
Blue if I wanted a gentle rocking.
I loved that part, poised
in front of the cabinet
at the moment of theft,
*eeny, meeny, miny, moe,*
my heart pounding so loudly
I thought for sure she'd hear.
And then the plunge into Mother's
strange dreamless sleep.

# Another Spring

*Is there a term in any language for choosing to be happy?*

—Ellen Bass, "The Small Country"

# Even an Angel

Branches *shush* the house,
ambient light mutes
an extravaganza of stars.

I climb from bed
and stand by the window
where an opinionless dark

comforts me. Slowly,
light, and from the highest
branch of a white pine

a cardinal's vivid
two-world call. I'm thinking
life deserves a cardinal at the top of every tree

when he swoops down, a sudden
fire in the blackberry bush—
even Rilke's angel is startled by the tang.

# Mother's Day

All of New York must be outside today, the first day
the sun has any strength at all, and I want to take her to the park

but already she's angry at me for suggesting the wheelchair.
*How is it,* she says, *I do so well when you're not here?*

I'm not going to answer that. I'm going to pile our purses
into the wheelchair—*just in case*—and maneuver it with one hand

and give her my other arm to lean on. We weave our way
toward the park, a walk that would be a lot easier

if she'd just sit in the wheelchair, which she won't, folding herself
instead onto a bench. We watch taxis blaring by. We breathe buses.

*It's just another few blocks to the pond,* I say cheerfully,
thinking of the model boats with their brisk white sails,

children intent on the controls. *I grew up here,* she says.
*I know what the pond looks like.* And so we head back,

the same off-kilter walk as I try to steer the wheelchair
and keep ahold of her. I'm concentrating so hard

it's a surprise, as we round the corner at 74th Street,
to come upon a profusion of white lilies

planted around a tree. How could we have missed that?
*I remember these flowers,* she says. She does?

She stares at the lilies and moves close, so close
I wonder if she's going to gather them in her arms,

or pick a few choice blooms to take home.
But she just looks, and smells, and smiles.

I turn her body so the sun isn't shining in her eyes.
*What are you doing?* she says, pulling away.

*You're beautiful,* I say. *I'm taking your picture.*
She draws herself up a little taller, angles her chin

in a take-charge way. She looks right at me.
I have it now, a picture of my mother with lilies.

# *Walking to the 58th Street Library*

The first block stretched on with big doors
and sometimes a doorman standing in front
who smiled or touched his hand to his hat
and I hurried past to get to the next block
where the houses were smaller and pressed
close together and each one had its own set of steps
leading to a front door. And I wanted to run up
and down those steps. All of them. And my mother

waited while I ran up, she waited while I ran down.
She wasn't in a hurry. And when I flew into her,
pleased with myself and a little out of breath,
she took my hand in her cool fingers
and we started walking again, as if she were rich
in time, and I was what she wanted to spend it on.

# In the Small Rotary

where Route 100 meets School Street,
two cows graze. I've heard Vermonters
lend their cows to neighbors—and to the city,
it seems—free food for cows, free mowing
for the field's owner. But a rotary?
That hardly seems like a field to me. And
they must stop traffic, those cows, whatever
traffic there is, when they're led in and out
of the makeshift enclosure. I picture a farmer
trying to hurry his cows—
how do you hurry cows? With a birch switch?
Or is that for punishing kids? I seem to remember
you have to stay calm with cows. And
where is the gate, anyway? I circle several times,
searching for a break in the wire fencing,
when my cell phone rings. I pull over
to take the call, keeping an eye on the postcard
perfect scene, dappled black and white cows,
trees budding into lacy green in the hills beyond.
It's my mother, telling me she's just had dinner
with Ralph Waldo Emerson. *What's he like?*
I ask. *Pretty narcissistic,* she says. The cows
keep grazing, looking content in their
miniature field. My mother goes on—
*I really couldn't stand how he insisted
on his own opinion. So what did you do?*
I ask. *I didn't do anything,* she says. *I left the arguing
to Thoreau.* Is it worth the farmer's time,
I wonder, to herd them here, and then

to herd them home? *Thoreau was there too?*
I ask. *Yes, of course. Emerson, and Thoreau.*
*The two of them kept at it, each one trying to prove*
*he was right, or at least prove the other one wrong.*

# At the Feeder

In a flurry of wings
sparrows fight for a place.
Finches puff themselves up to keep warm.

On a branch of the blue spruce
a woodpecker struts his stuff—
speckled belly, striped wings,

that fiery head. I wait for him
to come closer, to drum on the suet
where I can watch the choreography

of desire, or need, play out before me,
stripped of the bafflement of words.
And when I look away

the woodpecker does fly to the feeder—
minutes later, when I look back, he's there.
Why not, for once, or always, err on the side of joy?

# Minor Key

I'm walking to the reservoir, tuned to a vague
creak of branches, the give of pine needles,
while the puppy runs ahead, barking at moss,
at mushrooms breathing like a distant highway.
Now she skitters into a brook and barks at water,

when, with a fearful flapping, a wild turkey
lands in our path. And stays there, unmoving.
That Vizsla, my flap-eared protector, makes a wide circle
and leaps, whimpering, into my arms. Whatever story
I'll make of this day, hugging my knees around a campfire

of the soul, it will be that leap, purple bruises
hammered into my chest. The dog's snuffling, trying
to make herself smaller. With bears, you ring bells
or shout to scare them off. Does noise work with a turkey?
I don't like the look of those spurs on the back of its legs.

The head seems to be changing color, from grey
to red. That couldn't be a good sign. I should turn
and walk slowly away. But there's a prehistoric dignity
to this creature, throat adorned with great grey carbuncles,
webbed wattles under the chin. Who knows

what we should be afraid of, or why. Those wings—
iridescent green with streaks of copper, opening
into a courtesan's fan, a thief's cloak, wry, elegant,
raucous, an invitation, an announcement—those wings
celebrate themselves, a minor key Brandenburg concerto.

# Call and Response

We're canoeing the Boundary Waters
in northern Minnesota, my daughter
in the stern, a nautical map
open on her knees. She steers us
toward the east end of the lake
while I watch for danger
from the bow. I'm good at this.
*Rocks!* I shout. *Fallen tree!*
She avoids rocks and fallen trees
and guides us to the portage,
slick with mud from yesterday's
downpour. I hoist on my pack
and keep my eyes on the path,
watching for slippery roots,
unsteady stones. Red flag
of hair escaping her bandana,
Abby carries our canoe
upside-down on her shoulders.
*Beaked hazel,* she calls to me.
*Bunchberry. Spotted coralroot.*

# Crystal Reflections Halo the Moon

The world becomes vast.
The vast becomes worldly.
Whirling through space, I'm
stilled, dizzy with the vast
world.  My heart beats

in my mouth. My breath stops
and starts. I stare. Staring,
I start. It's risky to start.
Today, in the woods, I found
houndstooth and bleeding heart,

mixed them with a handful
of chamomile. I worked backwards,
breadcrumbs losing their way
in the creases of my tablecloth.
Never cut challah with a knife,

it's an instrument of war.
Though tearing the bread
also seems barbaric—
those jagged edges. Stars
intrude around me. Or luck

has little to do with it.
I'm tinged with the invisible,
dusted with lust. I shake out
my hair and point to the moon.
Not as a place. As enough.

## *The Public Garden*

The sun is shining and I'm content
to be myself, walking across the Common
as families queue up by the Swan Boats,

real swans parting the water
in elegant wakes. *This is*
*la vie en rose—*

on a lawn vivid with spring
people walk their dogs, peeling off
in clusters of introduction and gossip;

below a sign that shouts *Don't*
*Feed the Ducks,* families throw
wadded-up bread into the pond;

kids on the carousel want
*More! More!* Frisbee players,
tourists in Red Sox caps, babies

with their dimpled elbows,
the guy on stilts, the pretzel vendor,
the woman holding out a cup for change

as she recites our forecast,
I'm taking it in, all of it, sun
and melting cones, skinned knees

and soothing words
and single shining tears,
whatever love has rained on us all.

# *Acknowledgments*

Grateful acknowledgment is made to the editors of journals in which these poems first appeared, sometimes in earlier versions, sometimes with different titles.

*The Bellingham Review:* "Arrivals (iii)";
*Blue Lyra Review:* "Favorite Uncle," "Storm";
*Cerise Press:* "Lullaby," "Three Lives";
*The Comstock Review:* "Crimson Peonies," "Fax from My Son";
*Connotation Press:* "Central Park," "Midsummer Opera";
*The Delmarva Review:* "Chimes," "First Child," "Grandson, Just
        Born," "Monday Morning," "My Grandmother's Clock,"
        "Nights";
*Kenning Journal:* "Long Shadows," "Why Is This Night Different?";
*Literary Mama:* "Call and Response," "Mornings," "Woolen Hat";
*Mom Egg Review:* "Constellations";
*Nimrod:* "My Mother Turns Ninety";
*Prairie Schooner:* "The Print above My Bed";
*Prime Number:* "Cats";
*Salamander:* "Another Last Summer," "In the Small Rotary,"
        "Walking to the 58th Street Library";
*Solstice:* "At Twelve," "Boardwalk Rhapsody," "The Gods,"
        "Russian Novel," "Taffeta. Lipstick. Stockings.,"
        "Questions, 1969";
*Tar River Poetry:* "Still Life," "Without Dog";
*Valparaiso Poetry Review:* "Lizard";
*West Branch:* "As the Fog Burns Off," "Hoopla."

"Frankincense," as "The Letter," was included in *Lay Bare the Canvas: New England Poets on Art.* The Poetry Loft, Cranston RI, 2014.

Line from "The Small Country," poem by Ellen Bass, copyright ©
2015, used by permission of the author.

"Crimson Peonies" is in memory of Marsha. "Russian Novel" is
for Ivy. "Another Last Summer" is for Rena. "Lizard" is for Missy.
"Cats" is for Julia and Sophia.

Thanks to Barbara Helfgott Hyett for being my sister-friend in po-
etry. Thanks to Anne Fowler for turning up in Kinereth Gensler's
poetry class thirty years ago. Thanks to my friends in the Monday
morning free write group for searching, together, for the unexpect-
ed. Thanks to Steve Huff and Phil Memmer at Tiger Bark Press for
their belief in my poetry and for giving this book a home. Thanks
to The Writers' Room of Boston, for being there. And thanks to
Team Mnookin for reminding me what can be created with crayons
and glue. For showing up, with humor, energy, dogs, tech support,
Paleo brownies, patience, and love.

# About the Author

Wendy Mnookin is the author of four previous books of poetry, *The Moon Makes Its Own Plea* (2008), *What He Took* (2002), and *To Get Here* (1999), from BOA Editions, and *Guenever Speaks* (1991), a book of persona poems. The recipient of an NEA Fellowship in Writing, she has published poems in *The Delmarva Review, Nimrod, Prairie Schooner, Salamander,* and *Solstice,* among other journals, and in anthologies, including *Boomer Girls: Poems by Women from the Baby Boom Generation,* and *Urban Nature: Poems about Wildlife in the City.* Her work has been featured on *Poetry Daily* and on Garrison Keillor's *The Writer's Almanac.* Mnookin has taught poetry in the Boston area at Emerson College, Boston College, and Grub Street, a non-profit writing program, and at writing workshops around the country. She lives with her husband in Newton, Massachusetts, where they raised their three children. Her website is at www.wendymnookin.com.

# Colophon

The text of *Dinner with Emerson* is set in Aparajita,
with titles in Adobe Caslon Pro.

This trade edition of *Dinner with Emerson*
was printed by BookMobile in Minneapolis, MN.
Twenth-six copies were numbered and signed by the author
for presentation purposes.
This copy is Number:

Publication of this book was made possible
through the generous contributions of the following donors:

Michael Ansara
Ellen and David Blumenthal
Shira Goodman and Wes Gardenswartz
Molly and Jeff Goodman
Ezra Gut
Sherry and Ned Holstein
Roger Driben and Nancy Kane
Rabbi Lifson Library
Mike and Linda Lyon
Hal Poster and Susan Miller
Laura Stamas and Abigail Mnookin
Bob and Dale Mnookin
Jacob and Isabel Mnookin
Seth and Sara Mnookin
Susan and Jim Sidel
Paul and Betsy Sittenfeld
Ellen Waterston
Claudia Weill

## More Poetry from Tiger Bark Press